Book two of the
Divine Dark Feminine
series
Exploring the path
of
the ancient goddess
in a modern world

ERESHKIGAL

BY

SCOTT IRVINE

In memory of
Carolyne Jane Ann Hopps
30/11/62 - 29/9/83

All rights reserved,
no part of this publication
may be either reproduced
or transmitted
by any means whatsoever without the
prior permission of the publisher.

VENEFICIA PUBLICATIONS UK
veneficiapublications.com
Typesetting © Veneficia Publications

Text & Ereshkigal artwork © Scott Irvine

UK January 2021
Edited by Veneficia Publications
&
Fi Woods
Cover artwork © Scott Irvine 2021

CONTENTS

1	INTRODUCTION
2	THE QUEEN OF DEATH
9	INTO THE UNDERWORLD
16	DIVIDE AND CONQUER
21	THE LIGHT OF HIDDEN KNOWLEDGE DAWNING IN THE DARKNESS OF CREATION AKA THE DARK QUEEN OF DEMONS ROAMING IN THE MEADOW OF DELIGHTS
25	THE INNER DEMON
31	THE BIGGER PICTURE
35	EVOKING THE DARK GODDESS
38	A CIRCLE OF TRANSFORMATION AND REBIRTH
42	A SIMPLE RITUAL FOR A TIME OF BEREAVEMENT
43	A RITUAL FOR STRENGTH IN TIMES OF DIFFICULTY
44	A DEVOTIONAL TO ERESHKIGAL

INTRODUCTION

The feminine goddess, both the dark and wanton harlots and the grieving mother - all have a place not only in the world but within each and every one of us: our shadow side, our lost moments, regrets, resentments and heartaches. The dark and divine feminine exists in all of us and has always done so.

This book explores some of those darker emotions, that come with the heartache of loss, whether thrust upon us or of our own doing heartbreak has affected or will affect us all in some way.

Ereshkigal is no stranger to grief and loss. She does not condemn our sorrow, our rage, or our inability to cope. Instead, through her own heartache she shows us that grief is something which can bring a deeper understanding of the continuation of life, and how death is an essential part of our spiritual journey. Though painful, grief can bring about the change needed to heal our emotional scars.

Diane Narraway

THE QUEEN OF DEATH

Ereshkigal sat patiently alongside the seven Anunnaki judges, waiting for her sister to arrive from the land of the living. Her mood, like her influence across the three worlds, was dark. Ereshkigal's sister, Ishtar, was Queen of the Heaven in the Upperworld, Queen of the Earth in the Middleworld, and was now on her way to claim Ereshkigal's Underworld realm too. Only over Ereshkigal's dead body would that ever happen. The Underworld had been the Dark Queen's domain ever since she was old enough to manage the realm herself.

It was a decree made by the 'Lord of the Earth', Enki, that she replaces her father, the 'Moon God' Sin from being born in the subterranean world; a realm that housed the souls of the dead after a life in the land of the living.

All because her grandfather Enlil, the 'Lord of the Air' had forced himself on his cousin the grain goddess Ninmah, impregnating her with the seed of the Moon God, she was the one punished to run the affairs of the disembodied human spirits at the heart of 'Mother Earth.' Just so the Moon could shine in the night sky alongside the planets and stars for the Earth to gaze upon and wonder.

Ever since humanity learnt to make their own tools, they were aware of an invisible force within nature that gave them everything they needed to exist. For them, this energy came from Mother Earth, guiding them to live in harmony with the land, where nature was seen as proof of the god and goddess working together to create life. At death, the Stone-Agers understood that the human spirit would return to the womb of the mother goddess; she had protected them in life, now she comforted them in death, and prepared them for the next stage of their existence.

Then the Anunnaki arrived, a patriarchal dominant influence that transformed the three worlds to their own design. They ruled from the Upperworld of Heaven over humanity in the realm of the Middleworld, who were enchanted to build cities and temples to honour them; electing Kings and priests to carry out the will of the new rulers of Earth.

Ninmah, pregnant with the Moon God demanded that she went with the father of her unborn child into the underworld; she loved Enlil and refused to be without him when he was ordered by his brother Enki to reside in the 'Halls of Death' as punishment.

Her wish was granted, but it caused great concern for the ruling gods that the Moon, destined to rule the night sky of the heavens, would be born in the darkness of death, and would only be seen by those passing through to the next life. Enki could not have that; it would ruin the plans of his father, Anu, the king of the gods and goddesses on Earth. Enki commanded that Ninmah be released, but she would only leave if Enlil could join her above ground. It was a hard bargain, but Enki agreed on the decree that upon coming of age, the first born of Sin would become the permanent ruler of the underworld and manage the affairs of the dead for the rest of time.

To Ereshkigal, it was outrageous that she was serving her grandfather's punishment so her father could light up the night sky and rule over the other heavenly planetary influences as Enlil's heir. She had been destined to be the goddess of passion and lust, to balance the eternal love and compassion of her sister, Ishtar. By working together, the world would have been very different, but split between two realms their power was greatly diminished, allowing the masculine power of the God to gain control over the feminine energy for the first time in Earth's long history.

Ereshkigal hated to see humanity become slaves to civilisation, which she saw as nothing but a world of worker's creating Gods' heaven on earth. How could humanity be so blind as to be led like the cattle they herded for clothing and meat?

Ereshkigal's little sister, precious Ishtar was the Queen of everyone's heart and their young brother the radiant Sun God Shamash was prophet to both King and his subjects while she, through no fault of her own, inhabited the dark cold realm of the Underworld. It just was not fair.

The Queen of Death had no interest in caring for the disembodied souls that arrived in her kingdom; for all she cared they could rot in hell. Her realm, by all accounts, was sparse of any pleasure and void of love; it was a world sterile of anything good, and joy was as rare as an Ereshkigal smile.

The portal between the middle world of the living and the underworld of the dead is separated by seven impenetrable walls that can only be accessed by guarded gates allowing no human, dead or alive to pass through. For Ishtar, as the Queen of Heaven and Goddess of Love, it was simply a matter of relinquishing a piece of attire at each gate, permitting her to descend through all the gates to arrive at Ereshkigal's halls naked. She came in the name of Love: the eternal Love of her husband, Sin's cousin, the grain god Tammuz. The deadly claws of Ereshkigal had brought him to her infertile kingdom, enraging Ishtar to come and rescue the love of her life, even if it meant conquering the underworld and manipulating the laws of the universe. Standing outside the great hall, Ishtar called out to her sister inside:

'Open the door gatekeeper so that I may enter. If you refuse and not let me in, I will smash the door down and shatter the lock; I will destroy the door posts and remove the gates and raise up the dead who outnumber the living so they can eat the flesh of the people on the earth'.

Ishtar had threatened to unleash the first zombie holocaust into the world of the living if she did not get her way. The door swung open and the Goddess of Love stormed in to face her sister. When their eyes met; one set full of raging love and the other the gaze of instant death, the life spark of Ishtar was extinguished, and she fell lifeless to the ground. Death, on this occasion, was the stronger force and Ishtar's naked corpse was hung unceremoniously on a meat hook on the wall.

On the surface, nature began to wither and die; rains did not fall, and rivers did not flood their

banks. Crops failed, cattle refused to mate, and humanity became barren. The fertility of nature had disappeared from the world. Ereshkigal held the fate of the planet in her hands and used the situation to negotiate a better existence for herself; she felt the Gods owed it to her. When humanity reached the point of starvation, Lord Enki had to intervene, so he sent a eunuch to charm his nephew's daughter into resurrecting the fertility god and goddess

So that order on the surface could be restored, the deal was that Tammuz would return to Ereshkigal each autumn harvest for the winter and be released back to Ishtar each spring to fertilise the land when the Earth gradually grew warmer with Shamash's increasing strength. The dark queen felt a little cheated and became even more bitter and angry with the world. She had lost two full-time souls in exchange for one part-timer; where was the fairness in that? At every dark moon, in revenge, an angry Ereshkigal would visit the living world with her demons, releasing her lust and passion on any man she came across, leaving him dead and returning to the underworld with his pathetic soul.

The powerful force of love, as they say, arrives when you least expect it and it was no different for Ereshkigal. The thought of love disgusted the dark goddess, but life changed when she sent an ambassador to heaven in her place for a feast for Anu.

The God of War, Nergal,

refused to stand on occasion for the Dark Queen's representative, which was duly reported when he returned to the Underworld. Ereshkigal was furious and demanded the impertinent god join her in the realm of the dead. Undeterred, the god of Mars marched into the Underworld with fourteen of his best warriors to take control and keep open the seven great gates to hell. Nergal stormed into the palace, found the ambassador that reported him, and killed him without a second thought. Then the God of War found his niece Ereshkigal on her throne at his mercy. For the first time in her life, Ereshkigal felt helpless and burst into tears, dropped to the floor on her hands and knees begging for the war god's mercy. Nergal advanced, raising his sword to cut off her head, when the Dark Queen offered him marriage and control of the subterranean kingdom of the dead. Nergal lowered his sword, dried Ereshkigal's tears, and accepted her offer. Nergal had a kingdom to rule and Ereshkigal, with much work to be done around the place, had a husband who could repair and make things. It was a match made in Hell, with a love that came from Heaven.

INTO THE UNDERWORLD

We have all experienced death in one form or another. We're constantly surrounded by it on television and in the media, and only the most hard-hearted would not feel sadness and despair. Many of us have personally lost a family member, a close friend or loyal pet, leaving us distraught and heartbroken. It is a fundamental truth that one day, each and every one of us will die and our spirits will begin new existences in a different realm that follows death.

Ereshkigal creeps in the shadow between life and death, invisible to those unaware of her existence. She is an ancient goddess from the time when our hunter gatherer ancestors were transforming into civilised humans, between the two mighty rivers of the Euphrates and Tigris in Mesopotamia. Her kingdom is a realm where nothing happens; there is no change or growth. It's a world where thick dust settles, stifling any life before it can even exist. It is a lifeless world, where only rats and worms have a generous existence, growing fat off the decaying flesh of dead bodies.

Ancient Sumerian and Babylonian texts describe how the

Underworld became the residency for the lower half of the Mother Goddess Tiamat, when she was cut in two by Enki's son Marduk. Since the separation from her higher self, Tiamat, once the womb of life became a hell hole of death and decay hidden deep within the Earth.

Everything above the Earth's surface was the Queendom of Ishtar and what was beneath belonged to Ereshkigal, a subterranean realm called Huber, which she ruled with her husband Nergal. The ancient texts reveal that Ereshkigal ruled over three levels of subterranean worlds, known as Halls. The upper level is the Hall of Amenti, a five-star hotel if you like, for the gods and goddesses to rest and recover from the constant cycle of change and transformation of the Middleworld. It is also known as the Great Hall, where the river of life flows, nourishing the womb of Mother Earth. It was once the residence of the spirits of our Stone-Age ancestors, who understood that death was a portal to a rebirth in a new reality of consciousness. With civilisation came humanity's fall into the lowest level of existence at death, while the gods took over paradise and power over death as well as life.

The middle level is the Hall of the Living, where a flower of fire grows, driving away the darkness of death. Its

radiance of eternal light is the spirit of life that restores health and heals suffering. In the basement level sits the Hall of the Dead, once reserved for the evil demon spirits and sinners, but now the realm for all human spirits after death. It is a rundown, dark world with only the basic
requirements necessary to sustain consciousness. Well, that is what the Babylonian priests would have us believe. One thing for sure, is that one day we will all find out the truth of the matter.

    I was bought up to believe that if I was good throughout my life I would go to heaven and if I was bad, I would go to Hell. Heaven is a paradise where we would rest eternally with our loved ones in bliss and Hell was a realm of fire and brimstone, starvation and eternal torture, ruled by the Devil according to Christianity.

    Through Marvel comics and the like, I was introduced to the gods and goddesses of the Vikings; like Thor, Odin, and Loki and found their realm of the dead much more interesting.

    Their paradise of heaven was reserved for those killed in glorious battle; the bravest heroes chosen by Odin's Valkyries led by Freya, the goddess of love and war. Existence in heaven, or Valhalla, for them was spent eternally drinking beer, fighting, and making love to beautiful women. A great afterlife for men, but as I have said, you need to die a hero's death on the battlefield, which is unlikely for most of us in today's world. For the likes of you and me, who will most probably die naturally, accidentally, or through an illness, will have to travel to the frozen north to reside in a cheerless bliss with the queen of the underworld, Hel.

The Hindu Indians believe in something called 'karma', which means that the way we live our lives determines whether we go to a blissful heaven with Yama and our ancestors and loved ones until the end of time or are sent to the realm of the twenty-one hells. Here, judgement is made before reincarnation into a good or bad existence in a fresh body and a new life on Earth.

In other words, the more compassionately you lead your life, the more harmonious your next life will be.

Whatever death is, whether a portal to a new existence or an eternal sleep, we will all find out in due course. There is not anything we can do about dying, so there really is no point worrying about it; just enjoy life for what it is and be the best person that you can be. We tend to fear death because we are left behind without knowing where our loved ones have gone. We suffer the loss badly because for us, they have gone forever, and we

grieve and cry because we miss them; it leaves a hole in our heart. It is the process of grief that comforts us through the sadness; a grief that is the embodiment of Ereshkigal, who can ease our suffering, opening the way for sadness and acceptance allowing the frail human mind to cope.

It was a damp autumn morning in 1983, close to the Celtic hillfort 'Badbury Rings', deep in the Dorset countryside when a pretty young woman, weeks away from her 20th birthday, fell off her motorbike into the path of an oncoming car. She died instantly. Her name was Carolyne and she was the love of my life. Days earlier, we were looking at flats to move into and engagement rings, preparing to spend the rest of our lives together; but in an instant she was gone forever. My young mind, fresh from completing my apprenticeship, was not equipped to deal with it and I quickly spiralled downwards into a world of drink and drugs that helped to release me from the hurt and pain. I was angry and took to fighting in pubs and pulling women in nightclubs; a rebel without a cause with no care for myself or those around me. I soon lost my job and any respect for anything disappeared into a drunken haze of anarchy and chaos. That was my world for around six months, until good friends and family thankfully got through to me that it was not what Carolyne would have wanted; their help ensured that my visit to Hell was a short one. I grew to like the idea that Carolyne was now my guardian angel and was looking over me, keeping me safe and protected from harm. I still had many unanswered questions that no one could answer; why did she have to die so young? Why should I have to suffer such a great loss, when all my friends were beginning to settle down and have families? Why me? I was not satisfied with the response that I got from the church, so I went in search of the answers myself.

I began a philosophy course where I was amazed to learn that I had two bodies, one of flesh and one of spirit, and everything from the spirit world was only a projection of our minds through our five senses. Everything that exists in the universe, both physically and spiritually, is energy in different forms with different wavelengths that are constantly changing into something else and could never be destroyed. Carolyne's body was dead and buried, but her spirit or soul, the essence of who she was, still existed as a new life form in a new realm or dimension. I learnt that wherever she is, it is a happier place than this one of constant antagonism from the 'Four Horsemen of the Apocalypse'.

Creeping in the shadows ensuring that life continues, despite death, is

Ereshkigal, who pierces through the illusion that is life. She is the raw, primal dark force who takes the human spirit at death and prepares them for their new futures. The Goddess of Death, through the grieving process, enables those left behind to overcome the sadness and hurt in their hearts by planting a seed that will grow in the darkness into loving memories of the departed love one.

DIVIDE AND CONQUER

Before the Anunnaki gods arrived here, around 450,000 years ago, at the beginning of the Stone Age, humans worked together for the benefit of everyone to ensure their survival. Tribes migrated across the globe in search of food, shelter, water, and security that they believed was provided by the powerful forces of Mother Earth and Father Sun. Our early ancestors saw these two forces generating the life that was nature, from which everything that they required existed.

The Stone Age goddess, the Sumerian texts reveal was a great mass of sea water called Tiamat, the 'Mother of Life', who floated in an abyss of nothingness, asleep. Within her mass were all the ingredients for creating life; she was sacred. No one knows how long Tiamat drifted alone in the abyss, as there was no time or space then, but she was stirred into wakefulness when she felt a pull on her mass from something separate from her. She was attracted to this new energy drawing her closer, causing her heart to race and her waters to warm up and become agitated. Tiamat felt ecstatic and called this feeling 'Love'.

The energy she was drawn to was Apsu, the 'Father of Abundance', a boundless vastness of pure fresh water that was attracted to Tiamat, coming together to become one powerful force. From out of their love for one another a new third energy was created, an energy called Mummu, a mist of chaos that contained both the sea and pure waters of his parents. From out of the chaos came Father Heaven, the god Anu; Mother Sky, the goddess Antu and Mother Earth, the goddess Ki.

With Antu, Anu fathered the elder Enki, the Lord of the Sea, and with Ki, Anu produced his heir, prince Enlil, the God of the Air.

As the royal family grew, they got louder and rowdier, causing such a racket that they began to annoy Apsu. Eventually Mummu and the Father God decided enough was enough and prepared a plan to destroy all of their offspring on Earth. Tiamat agreed that their children needed to be punished but was against destroying them and refused any part of the plan, warning Enki what was coming. Enki was a very powerful wizard and, as Lord of the Earth, used his magic to enchant Apsu into a deep sleep, stealing his fresh rain and river waters for himself. He chained Mummu to Apsu and had them imprisoned in a deep cave under an island, off the west coast of the European continent. On hearing the sad news, the Moon god Sin, the son of Enki's brother Enlil and the chief planetary god, urged Tiamat to seek retribution on his uncle. It was not long before Tiamat was leading an army of demons towards Earth, to exact revenge for the loss of her husband and son Mummu.

Enki offered his son Marduk the kingdom of Earth, if the young warrior prince stopped and defeated the she-dragon in her tracks before she could destroy the royal family on Earth. The prince met his great-great grandmother and her hordes of demons at the edge of the solar system and offered her the chance to settle things in single combat. Tiamat agreed: winner takes all.

The battle was long and hard but eventually Tiamat began to tire against her younger opponent and Marduk quickly got the upper hand.

He cast his net, carried on the corners by the four winds, causing Tiamat to dive out of the way. She opened her great jaws to spray the royal prince with fire, but Marduk shot a flaming arrow into her mouth, igniting the gases of her stomach, triggering an explosion that ripped out her heart, killing her instantly.

After removing Tiamat's 'Tablets of Destiny' and placing them around his own neck, giving him the power to create the universe in his own image, Marduk cut the ancient mother in two. The new ruler of the universe cast Tiamat's top half to the furthest reaches of the heavens, imprisoning her sacred life-giving waters, so they could not return to Earth, and her lower half was imprisoned in the depths of the Earth, with her subterranean waters guarded by death and decay.

For his part in the attack, the Moon god Sin was stripped of his planetary kingship and transformed into a less powerful female family member. Sin's daughters were given the authority of minding the ancient influences of the Mother Goddess: Ishtar reigning over her higher self, with Ereshkigal presiding over the lower half.

Tiamat had been divided in half and now, with her forces conquered, Marduk was free to administer his own laws on Earth: laws that ensured humans would serve God under the guidance of priests and kings. The human population would build temples to the gods and goddesses and live in controlled cities from now on. A new world order had begun; a world of conflict and division that humanity had never experienced before. The Mother Goddess was life and death, past and future, light and dark; now there was only life or death, past or future, light or dark. When the Mother was split in two, dis-harmony and dis-ease were born into the new civilised world of hierarchy and the ego grew to control the human mind. The minority

controlling powers found that by constantly dividing society, they could easily keep the majority occupied with pride, arrogance, superiority, and self-importance leading to jealousy, fear and hatred. We quickly became slaves to the system.

By creating two opposing sides as in politics, religion and sport to name a few, we give rise to competition where winners and losers are made, leading to rivalry and conflict. In reality, we are all souls dwelling in a physical body, with the same needs, on the same planet, all relying on the same resources found in nature. To ensure the survival of the human race, we need to share our resources equally and live in peace with each other and nature.

THE LIGHT OF HIDDEN KNOWLEDGE DAWNING IN THE DARKNESS OF CREATION AKA THE DARK QUEEN OF DEMONS ROAMING IN THE MEADOW OF DELIGHTS

Light and dark are opposing forces of the same power: light is energy that is bereft of dark and dark is energy devoid of light. The simplest way to find light is in the darkness where it cannot hide. In the light, there is always darkness hidden in the shadows; likewise, in the dark, there is always a glimmer of light veiled in the gloom. It is the darkness that gives light its power. Like the sisters Ereshkigal and Ishtar, one cannot exist without the other. Without death, life cannot exist; equally, death cannot exist without life. Without the opposing forces that our reality consists of, change would not happen, and fertility could not sustain nature. Unless Ereshkigal destroys matter, Ishtar is unable to create anything new. The sisters are the most efficient recyclers on the planet and without the death or destruction of something, change cannot take place and evolution cannot occur.

I see Ereshkigal as the transformer that makes change happen; she is the destroyer of old things, enabling the birth of new ideas and thinking, new inspirations and beliefs, and new understanding and purpose. Without change the world would stop evolving, humanity would stagnate, and life would be meaningless. Imagine life as a book, where the writing of it is its conception and its release is the birth; its story is its life, and the ending is its death and rebirth. Without an ending to the story, the book would be pointless: incomplete and mind-numbing for anyone with the time to read it. Without an ending, the book will never be finished and never ready for release, because it will always be at the writing stage.

Working with the raw, primal, dark force of Ereshkigal, for me at least, is to maintain the balance of our existence, in order to bring harmony to a troubled world that appears to be constantly at war with itself. Through the Queen of Death, negative forces journey into the world of light, forcing change by attracting and repelling energy at an atomic level. This creates new forces in the physical world of space, time, and gravity: a conventional trinity from which duality exists.

There can be no secrets in the light because everything is visible. It is in the darkness that true knowledge is discovered, where light shines brightest. By using the cosmic dance between

Ereshkigal and Ishtar, the light will always hunt the darkness as day ceaselessly chases night and life continually pursues death.

I am a druid wearing a witch's hat: a biker, philosopher, and photographer with a fascination for ancient history. I am an active member of the Association of Portland Archaeology, which inspired my interest for the Stone Age Goddess. Who was she and how did our nomadic ancestors honour her?

When I can, I like to meditate in the ruin of Portland's oldest church; St. Andrews, close to where I live. The old site sits above a cliff, overlooking the sea; between the church and the cliff is the old cemetery that, as children, we called the 'Pirates' Graveyard' because of the skull and crossbones insignia on many of the headstones. It is an enchanting place to just sit and relax, listen to the wildlife in the elms, sycamores, and ash trees surrounding the ruin and feel the place shake as great waves hit the cliffs below on a stormy day. What I like about graveyards is that they are generally quiet places and usually void of people. My romance for cemeteries, though, was lost for some time twelve years ago, when I worked as a grave digger for the Council. Each new grave had to be dug by hand because machinery could not get near them. Unfortunately, I had to fill in a fresh

grave next to Carolyne's and the infill had been piled on top of her plot. I went crazy seeing her space covered in soil. It was general practice, as the graves were so close together and I had no problem before, but when it is someone you love, it felt wrong. I tried to carry on because the new corpse deserved my respect; after all they were someone else's loved one, but I found it all too difficult to bear, threw my shovel across the cemetery and quit my job. Obviously, I still had issues, even after twenty-five years my grieving was still not finished.

THE INNER DEMON

I am the raven with a message from the goddess. I will whisper it to you in your dreams when the portal to the spirits is open.

We've all heard that inner voice: that whispered message revealing our way forward in life and reminding us that the spirit world is watching over us and keeping us safe from danger. The nature of the inner voice, for me at least, always depends on the state of my outer reality: when I'm happy and everything is going good, the whole world is smiling but when I'm upset or annoyed, I feel that I am on my own. Recently, I have become aware that, during these uncertain times, with the arrogance of our government and local council, Brexit, and the coronavirus taking over the media, an unusual sense of wellbeing has been sneaking around in the shadow of my mind. It is an energy usually hidden in the darkness of the subconscious, now peeking out into the light of the consciousness for the first time.

That dark energy is Ereshkigal, the angel of death and the opposing force of the good and fluffy Ishtar, goddess of love and happiness. I found that by withdrawing into Ereshkigal, I was returning to the protective ancient womb of Tiamat, where my grief and sadness is processed and taken care of. By bathing in the comfort of her company, any unhappiness and misery simply dissolve into nothing, because Ereshkigal is the heartache that we find painful.

Ishtar is symbolised by the dove, the Holy Spirit of the trinity, where the Moon god Sin is the Father and the Sun god Shamash is the Son. Ereshkigal is represented by the raven, the scavenger that feeds on the decaying flesh of dead bodies cleaning the bones of flesh. Our Stone Age ancestors saw this as giving the body back to Mother Earth using the clean bones for worship and ritual. The raven is one of my favourite birds, alongside the blackbird and wren. In symbolic terms, the raven is the messenger and watcher of the gods and goddesses. They report what they witness on Earth back to their masters/mistresses and, on occasion, will reveal a divine message to a worthy individual. The bird represents the process of change: an inner journey of personal development. To personally encounter a raven is a signal that you are successfully moving forward along the path of life. When the raven speaks, you listen and when they perform for you, you take notice.

It was a windy overcast afternoon last autumn, when I was walking southwards towards the Bill along the west cliffs on Portland with my better half Therese. She pointed out a raven that was hovering just a few feet above us. I was convinced the bird would disappear by the time I got my camera out, but I was wrong. The raven gave me plenty of time to capture it in action, with its wings outstretched and its talons open, before landing at the edge of the cliff. We stopped to chat to the bird, as you do, letting it know how grateful we were for his time. We both asked for 'favours' in exchange for protecting nature and helping those worse off than ourselves.

When the raven had finished listening, it took off flying into the wind ahead of us, before gliding back past us. It made sure it caught our attention with an aerobatic display the red arrows would have been proud off, before flying ahead of us again and perching on the edge of the cliff waiting for us to catch up.

I knew the raven represented Ereshkigal from the research I did for my book '*Ishtar and Ereshkigal - Daughters of Sin*'. I saw its dance as a good omen despite the negative aspect of the goddess of death. Ereshkigal is change and progress that can only be achieved in the darkness. We stopped to chat again with our feathered friend. I felt

enlightened, wide awake, and connected to the whole universe at that moment. The wind was in our faces and the crashing waves below drowned out our senses as we connected to the raven again. The raven then flew effortlessly upwind along the cliff, turned and danced past us again on the wind, before flying ahead of us once more to land at Blacknor Point and wait for us to catch up again. The message I received was that all was well for us both, as a couple and individually. We had to both focus on the bigger picture to find the balance in our own lives; balance was the key and harmony was our fate. We thanked the raven and said our goodbyes before it rose into the sky, flew into the wind, raced past us again, swung inland into the quarry and out of sight.

    The raven played an important part in the Babylonian flood myth revealed in clay cuneiform tablets, discovered at the end of the nineteenth century from what is now Iraq. Ereshkigal's grandfather, Enlil, loved his peace and quiet, something he inherited from his great grandfather, Apsu. It's something most of us can appreciate: the bliss of quietness. With humanity migrating across  the whole planet, we became very rowdy and noisy, and the constant racket soon got under the Air god's skin. He decided enough was enough and set about destroying all of humanity with a great

biblical flood. Enki learned of the plot and warned his loyal priest Utnapishtim of the coming destruction and gave him plans to build a ship to carry the priest, his family, and the 'seed' of every living thing on the planet when the time came. The cuneiform texts reveal the craft was a perfect cube: a symbol of stability,
permanence, and geometric perfection, which represents the final stage in a cycle of tranquillity. Esoterically it is the squaring of a circle: a metaphor for bringing two things together, which are seen as so different that they should not exist as one thing. Think of Dali's 'Lobster Telephone'.

After six days and nights, the devastating storms weakened and on the seventh day the flood waters started to recede, exposing the ravaged Mesopotamian desert lands, now devoid of any life. Upnapishtim needed to find a fertile place to land, so that he and his family could revive the human race again. The old priest sent out a dove to search for life, but unable to find a place to roost, it returned to the ship before the day was out. After another seven days, a swallow was sent out and that also returned, unsuccessful at finding suitable land.
Another seven days later, a raven was sent out and this time the bird did not return, signalling to Upnapishtim that the bird had discovered fertile land nearby.

He steered the ship to land and marched, with his family and the 'seeds' of life he had bought with them, to the holy land that would sustain them long enough for his people to grow and re-populate the planet. After everyone had disembarked, a sacrifice was offered to the gods and goddesses who soon smelled the sweet aroma of burning flesh and came to give their blessings to all the survivors. All but Enlil that is, who was angry that any humans had survived at all.

THE BIGGER PICTURE

The most important factor for our continued existence on our planet is nature: a living, conscious entity we call 'Mother Earth' or 'Gaia'. She is the soil from which vegetation grows, allowing all creatures to feed and make shelter, also enabling humans to make tools and clothes. Without nature, we simply would not exist.

It is the Babylonian trinity that drives nature: Father Sin draws the subterranean water up to meet the roots at each full moon, his Son Shamash radiates light and warmth to feed the plants, which give oxygen for us to breathe. Ishtar with her opposing sister Ereshkigal ensure fertility and annual rebirth, so that nature can continue to grow and spread across the earth.

This process is vital for humankind to survive and allowing great swathes of forest to be cut down for concrete jungles and industry is immoral. It does nothing for the planet but cause pollution and make businessmen wealthy, all of which is detrimental to the people and animals that inhabit this planet. By destroying this vital source, we are sabotaging our continued existence. Mother Earth is dying and has been since the destruction of Tiamat, and the rise of the Kings and their empires 6,000 years ago.

Ereshkigal and Ishtar can be likened to the Chinese Yin and Yang, where Ereshkigal is Yin and Ishtar is Yang: opposing cosmic forces that create the change needed in the world for growth and development. Yin is darkness and is the below; she contracts, concludes, and receives. When our Yin nature is repressed, her dark influence turns us towards cruelty and corruption and encourages conflict with others; it is not wise to ignore our dark side.

To find the balance between the dark and light, we need to rise above our daily challenges and discover the fulcrum between the two opposing forces. This balancing point is never static and is always adjusting itself through the constant information it receives from the universe. To find the balance, it is important to hold both forces within your attention, seeing them together as a whole, seeing the positive and negative aspects equally. Embracing the balance allows you to see the bigger picture, helping you to find the wholeness that leads  to truth and harmony. Not everything is simply black and white: like most things there are many shades of grey in between. Like all opposites, there are many variations and proportions between the extremes that change constantly to be in tune with the universe. Taken individually, they are life or death, light or dark, and hot or cold. Together, they are rebirth, shade, and warmth.

Ereshkigal is the destructive force that allows change and renewal to occur, not only in physical things, but also in feelings and thoughts; this allows for new ideas to form. The goddess of death is the liberator that transcends limitations, boundaries, and obstacles, destroying old ways of thinking that no longer serve us. She is fearless and unconventional, residing outside the rationality of normal perception. Ereshkigal destroys negative feelings using her supreme dark force to absorb them at her will from your mind, but you have to understand the way she works you first have to allow her into your thoughts. Don't be afraid of her power; she understands the sorrow that comes from death, heartbreak, and loss because she is the primal force of sorrow. She can absorb the hurt from your heart if you allow her in to bathe in her darkness and wash away all your despair and sadness.

If you find a barrier or obstruction in your path, allow Ereshkigal to smash through it; she can do so with ease because she is all-powerful.

Hail the darkness, hail liberation from oppression: hail Ereshkigal.

EVOKING THE DARK GODDESS

The best place to discover Ereshkigal is in nature: the countryside, forest, park, or garden; anywhere there is vegetation. The further away from civilization and pollution, the better it is to just sit and be aware of where you are; be aware of the interaction of the elements through the five senses.

Relax and concentrate on your breathing, imagining the 'in' breath as the life force of Ishtar and the 'out' breath as Ereshkigal, a vapour that is poisonous to us, but vital for all the vegetation which in turn releases the oxygen that we need to breathe.

In ... and out.

In ... and out.

Fill your lungs with nature's gift that oxygenates your blood; it gives life to our cells and organs as it circulates the body, collecting toxins on its way and expelling them when we breathe out, giving life back to nature.

Breathe in stillness and breathe out tension. Feel gravity on your body pushing you down where you sit and be aware of the pressure under your feet on the ground and the earth under your feet.

Be aware of the clothes on your skin, the warmth of the covered body, and feel the air on your exposed skin. Notice the point where your clothing and exposed skin meet.

Allow your eyes to receive the colour and form of your surroundings, seeing Ereshkigal in the shadows of Ishtar's light. See everything as if it is for the first time.

Experience the taste in your mouth; smell your surroundings and the fresh air of nature.

Be fully *here* and aware of your central position in the universe at this moment in time.

Let sound flow into your mind: from the nearness of your breathing to the furthest, most distant, sound and everything in between. The more you listen, the more you hear.

Rest, experiencing this sense of awareness for as long as you are comfortable, before slowly returning to the mundane reality that is the thoughts and emotions of 'normal' life. Ground yourself by stamping your feet and shaking your hands. Your mind has been refreshed and recharged, and your body relaxed and rested. You are prepared and ready to carry on with life.

Ereshkigal is the destructive force that allows rebirth to occur, not only in the physical realm, but also in the spiritual world where our feelings and thoughts allow new ideas to form.

The Goddess of Death is transformation, the liberator who transcends limitations, boundaries, and most obstacles. She is fearless, compassionate, and unconventional. By destroying an old way of thinking because it no longer serves, you advance along the dark path of life following the light of Ishtar. Ereshkigal can destroy negative feelings because she is the supreme negative force, absorbing them at her will. Do not be afraid of her power; she understands the sorrow that comes from death and heartbreak of the loss of a loved one because she is the primal power of sorrow and heartbreak. Allow her to absorb your sorrow from your heart; all you have to do is ask. Bathe in her darkness to wash away your negative baggage.

Hail the darkness, hail destruction and hail Ereshkigal.

A CIRCLE OF TRANSFORMATION AND REBIRTH

Because of the dark nature of the goddess, the ceremony begins in the north and circles in the widdershins (anti-clockwise) direction.

'We call to the North: the direction of the dark sun and the element of Earth. We call to Sin, the King of the planets, bringing his knowledge and reflective insight within the darkness into the circle. Sin is all-powerful, generating the tidal forces on Earth and in us, producing mystery and magic.
Hail and Welcome.
We call to the West: the direction of the setting sun and the element of Water. We call to Ereshkigal, the evening star of Venus and queen of the Underworld bringing her transformative force into the circle. Ereshkigal is change and renewal after rest, transforming day into night.
Hail and Welcome.
We call to the South: the direction of the noon sun and the element of Fire. We call to Shamash, God of wisdom, bringing his fire of creation into the circle. Shamash is the God of light and heat, ensuring that water rises to the heavens to fall as rain.

Hail and Welcome.

We call to the East: the direction of the rising sun and the element of Air. We call to Ishtar, the morning star of Venus and Queen of Heaven, bringing her love and compassion into the circle. Ishtar is the freshness and wonder of a new day, transforming dark into light.
Hail and Welcome.'

The circle is now open for the presence of the Dark Goddess Ereshkigal, Lady of Death and destroyer of all things, so that new things can exist. She is the change in the universe: the transformer of all life.

She is the shadow cast by her brother, the Sun, on the brightest of days; she is the black velvet night where the stars and planets dance, and the creator of fiery endings and new beginnings. By her hand we are led from this life, so that our existence may continue in the spirit realm. Her mystery lies in the transformation of the life force, where only through death is life found anew. She is the goddess of revolution, and through her womb we shall all pass to find immortality. She is the strength that protects, comforts, and gives solace to those that need it at the time of death.

Remember her on dark moonless nights when she is most powerful. Trust in her and she will release you from your suffering and hurt. Blow her a kiss from the palm of your hand when the moon is dark, and she will smile on you, for she has been with you since the beginning and will remain with you at the end.

'Let us now share and enjoy magically crafted cakes.'

We offer our gratitude to the Dark Lady of Venus, where the light is reached through the dark of the womb. The food of the dead and the underworld is the food of the soul.

Let this cake be the symbol of the nourishing of your body and spirit, that we may be whole in both.

Into death does all life flow, to be refreshed and move into a new ever-flowing and never-ending life.

So, mote it be.
Closing the circle.

'From the North, we thank the reflective light of Sin in the night sky for his presence in our circle of rebirth. We also acknowledge the Earth, for keeping us grounded and allowing us to remain centered and connected to nature.

Hail and Farewell.

From the West, we thank the transforming nature of the Dark Queen Ereshkigal in the evening sky for her company in our circle of renewal. We also acknowledge the Water, for our rains that give nature her growth so that we can feed.
Hail and Farewell.
From the South, we thank the warming power of the god of light Shamash in the noon sky, for participating in our circle of regeneration. We also acknowledge the Fire, for his creative force that nourishes the human mind.
Hail and Farewell.
From the East, we thank the compassion and love of the Queen of Heaven Ishtar in the morning sky, for taking part in our circle of growth. We also acknowledge the Air for allowing us to breathe and the wind for transporting the seeds of nature to fresh ground.
Hail and Farewell.'

The circle is closed.

A SIMPLE RITUAL FOR A TIME OF BEREAVEMENT

Light a small candle or tea-light in a black or grey bowl. Place a small memento beside it of the person you are grieving for, preferably something that was worn next to their skin. Write something that you would like to say to that person, imagining them in front of you, as you do so. While holding the memento in your hand, burn the paper in the candle flame. As you watch it burn, imagine the message being delivered by Ereshkigal, to your loved one in her domain. Keep the memento on your person until you feel ready to put it away.

A RITUAL FOR STRENGTH IN TIMES OF DIFFICULTY

To invoke the Queen of Transformation for her strength, find a place that is safe and private, taking with you a feather from a raven or crow; Ereshkigal's sacred bird. Sitting comfortably, hold the feather in your hand, focusing your meditation on it. Take into consideration how its qualities can inspire the strength needed to overcome your current crisis.

Look deep into its darkness and imagine how you would like your life to be once the emergency is over.

Keep the feather in a safe place and whenever you feel your strength waning, take it out and remember what it represents to you. As you look at it, invoke Ereshkigal with the words:

'Ereshkigal, Queen of Transformation, lend me your strength to cope with the difficulties I now face.'

Blessed be.

A DEVOTIONAL TO ERESHKIGAL

Dark Queen Ereshkigal,
Allow me to rest in your
Darkness of deepest night,
Safe in your womb
where nothing can hurt.
Allow me to bathe
in your hidden realm
in the knowledge that I
am like a spark of light
free from time and open
to connect with All.

You are the death of illusion,
Of ignorance and suffering.
You are the rebirth
like an empty mind
ready to be nourished,
Awakened and fresh.

Cleanse me in the darkness
of Huber, your abode,
Where guests can recover,
Refresh and renew.
To experience the truth
that we are not body alone,
A suit we use to live

to interact with the world.
Your darkness reminds me
of the spirit we are,
The spirit we were
and the spirit we can become.
You are that I am.

You are the destroyer of ego,
Of self and personality,
A destroyer of illusion
that thrives in the light
of the false Gods of today.

Oh, Lady of Darkness,
Queen of the Night,
Faithful wife of Nergal,
The great God of War,
Who delivers bodyless souls
into your realm of decay
where all barriers to truth
are melted away.

In your deepest darkness
where I can swim in deep waters
that nourish the soul,
May I wash away my worries
that feed the fear of life
so, I can live in peace with myself,

and in harmony with nature
that allows us to be human,
And being human
as a human being
true to the higher self!

Scott Irvine © 2020

Scott Irvine is a druid and an active member and official photographer for the Cotswold Order of Druids.

He has followed the path of the goddess for over a decade, seeking her knowledge in both the light and darkness.

After contributing to several published by Moon Books including *Naming the Goddess* and *Seven Ages of the Goddess,* his first book *Ishtar and Ereshkigal - The Daughters of Sin* was released by them in March 2020.

He has recently contributed to the popular anthology Voices from the Ashes: Resurrecting the Wytch (Veneficia Publications October 2020).

He is also a regular contributor to Clan Dolmen Chronicles: a free online magazine aimed at the pagan, heathen and esoteric communities.

Scott lives on Portland in Dorset from where he recieves his inspiration to write.

Printed in the UK by CLOC Book Print
clocbookprint.co.uk

www.ingramcontent.com/pod-product-compliance
Lightning Source LLC
Chambersburg PA
CBHW071544080526
44588CB00011B/1786